Contents

A famous writer – *Shakespeare*

The whining schoolboy, with his satchel
And shining morning face,
creeping like snail
Unwillingly to school.

Do you know who wrote these humorous lines?
They were written more than 400 years ago, in a play called *As You Like It*.

The writer? William Shakespeare. Are you curious about this man? Want to know more?

1564 William was born in Stratford-upon-Avon. His parents were Mary Arden and John Shakespeare. He had seven brothers and sisters, but three of them died when they were children.

John Shakespeare was a glove maker and wool merchant, but it's likely that he did not know how to read or write. We think that his ambitious son, William, went to King's New School in Stratford, where he learned these skills.

In Shakespeare's time, there were more than 80 different ways of spelling his name.

Nobody knows Shakespeare's true birthday!

1582 William married Anne Hathaway, a farmer's daughter. He was 18 and she was 26.

1583 William and Anne had a baby girl, Susanna.

1585 Twins, Hamnet and Judith, were born.

An adventurous young man, William went to London to write plays and poems. London was a dangerous place, with many of its inhabitants suffering from serious diseases.

1593 A plague broke out in London and all the plays were cancelled.

1596 William's precious son Hamnet died, aged 11.

After these events, William wrote some of his darkest plays, like *Macbeth*, full of hideous happenings and murderous characters.

There are no relatives of Shakespeare living today – the last of his grandchildren died in the 1600s.

Actors say that it is bad luck to call the play *Macbeth* by its name. They call it 'the Scottish play'.

1599 The Globe Theatre opened in London, showing William's plays.

The Globe Theatre was destroyed by fire in 1613, but an updated Globe Theatre still shows Shakespeare's plays today. An episode of *Doctor Who*, starring David Tennant, was filmed there.

After writing numerous plays, William returned to Stratford.

1616 William Shakespeare died.

Shakespeare died on his 52nd birthday (or at least it is thought he did!)

In his will, Shakespeare left his 'second-best' bed to his wife, Anne. (His best bed was for guests.)

You are ...

a most villainous knave

a loathsome scab

like the toad,
ugly and venomous

foul and dangerous

a tedious fool

a man of wax

a puke-stocking

a poisonous, hunch-
backed toad

a jealous, rascally knave

a slug

a starved snake

a ravenous fish

Phrase	Meaning
a dish fit for the gods	a delicious dish
eaten out of house and home	eaten all my food
the green-eyed monster	jealousy
fight fire with fire	fight in the same way as your attacker
all that glitters is not gold	a pretty thing is not always valuable
a fool's paradise	happiness based on false hope

Mission impossible!

Terrible news has just come in from San Jose copper mine in Chile. An unstable roof has collapsed, leaving 33 miners trapped deep underground, unreachable.

The first rumblings above their heads told the miners that something was seriously wrong. They immediately fled to the emergency room, or refuge. There, nearly 700 metres below ground, foreman Luis Urzua began to organise his men.

When the dust cleared a group was sent out of the refuge to explore. What they found chilled their blood – huge rocks had left their escape route impassable. Next they tried the narrow, vertical ventilation shafts, but missing ladders made them unclimbable. They were trapped!

All they could do now was try to stay alive … and hope. Food was sensibly rationed, and drinkable water was taken from the radiators of stranded trucks. They used the trucks' batteries to power their head torches.

The heat was unbearable, and the men were faced with the challenge of staying healthy. One miner was made responsible for medicines. Although he wasn't trained, he had to treat injuries and illnesses. Their future unpredictable, they battled to keep each other's spirits up while they waited to be rescued.

Every two days each miner had to survive on:

- two spoonfuls of tuna
- one sip of milk
- half a cracker

Above ground, families watched and waited. They set up tents to live in, and local villagers brought them food. This new temporary home was named Camp Hope. Skilled engineers drilled narrow holes in the ground to try to locate the refuge, but as maps of the mine were unreliable, it was an almost impossible task. Then, on Day 17, a huge cheer echoed around the valley. Unbelievably, a drill had come back up to the surface with a note attached:

We are all well in the refuge.

The 33.

Supplies could now be sent down – bottled water, food and medicine, followed by a video camera. At long last the stranded miners were visible to the rest of the world. But could they be saved? And if so, how long would it take?

Scientists told the miners to switch lights off between 9 p.m. and 8 a.m. to try to simulate day and night. This would enable their bodies to keep to a normal daily routine.

A tiny projector was sent down so that the miners were able to watch Chile take on Ukraine in a live football match. Unfortunately Chile lost 2–1.

Now the engineers set about the considerable task of building a one-man escape capsule that could be lowered down to the miners. Space rocket experts gave advice, helping to create the life-saving device, named Fenix 2.

If Fenix 2 became trapped, a release catch would allow it to be lowered back down again

The miners had to shift the tons of rubble that fell as the drill hole was widened to allow Fenix 2 to pass. Finally it arrived, and one by one they began the 16-minute journey to freedom, squeezed uncomfortably into the capsule.

Each arrival at the surface was greeted with cheers as well as tears of joy. Luis Urzua was the last to leave the refuge. On 13th October, 69 days after disaster had struck, wearing sunglasses to protect his eyes, he stepped out of Fenix 2 to a hero's welcome. The most incredible rescue operation in history was complete.

Mission accomplished!

So what happened next?

Surviving over two months trapped underground earned the miners a place in the *Guinness Book of Records.*

Miner Edison Pena had kept himself fit by running nearly 10 kilometres a day through the tunnels. Just 25 days after his dramatic rescue, he took part in the New York Marathon. Still wearing dark glasses, and with ice strapped to his injured knee, he completed the course in 5 hours 40 minutes.

The miners' lives are likely to change forever. TV companies offered huge sums of money for interviews and to make programmes about the disaster. The miners made a formal agreement to share any money from films, books and interviews.

On 13th December, 23 of the miners were guests of honour at the football match between Manchester United and Arsenal. They were photographed with Manchester United legend, Sir Bobby Charlton, whose father was also a miner.

Pirate application pack

The pirate ship *Fresh Blood* is in the process of recruiting a new crew.

Interested?

Then please read this helpful information before sending in your application.

Qualifications

You must be young, fit, strong, not afraid to break the law and willing to fight. Education is not necessary, and a criminal record may actually help your application! All applicants must be male.

Pirates had many superstitions, one of which was that females brought bad luck on board a ship.

Job description

During periods of calm you will be required to:

- ☠ patch up sails damaged by cannonball fire
- ☠ make and mend ropes
- ☠ seal any cracks between planks with hot tar to keep the ship watertight
- ☠ keep your weapons clean and ready to use.

Bored pirates would get irritable, and then trouble would often start. In their spare time pirates would sing, dance or carve wooden ornaments. They would also play cards and dice, but gambling was banned as it caused fights.

When fighting against another ship, you will be expected to:

☠ obey instructions from the captain, without exception

☠ fight to the death.

Your rights

As a valued crew member, you will have a vote in the election of the captain, and also in any decision on whether or not to attack an enemy ship. You will receive your fair share of gold, silver or any other treasure following a successful raid.

Piracy was hardly a steady job. Pirates didn't know if their next trip might be their last. Once ashore in a friendly port it was quite common for pirates to spend all their share of the treasure in a single night, on luxuries such as fine food and drink.

Regulations

☠ You shall not attempt to run away in the heat of battle.

☠ You shall not strike another crew member.

☠ You shall not steal from another crew member.

In the event of such regulations not being obeyed, you will be put in front of a court consisting of your fellow crew members. If found guilty, the following punishments may be applied:

- ☠ confiscation of shares in treasure
- ☠ marooning on a desert island with just one bottle of water and a small supply of food
- ☠ walking the plank.

Provisions

Information on diet will be provided once the applicant is at sea.

It's not surprising they didn't want to go into details about food. A pirate's diet was, for the most part, disgusting. Although fresh fish could be caught on occasion, most meals consisted of mouldy meat and hard tack. This was a tough, dry biscuit – very likely infested by weevils and nibbled by rats. Water was stale and virtually undrinkable.

Dress regulations

A shirt, waistcoat and three-quarter length trousers are the usual uniform, with bare feet. Waistcoats may be coated with tar as added protection against swords.

Accommodation

'Compact' and 'cosy' are descriptions that have been supplied by previous successful applicants.

Compact and cosy? Well, I suppose that's one way of putting it. Pirates' living conditions were disgraceful. Crammed in like sardines, they never washed, so the place would be a dark, stinking pit. Rats would roam freely, and any disease spread quickly.

Health care

Due to the nature of the job, the management cannot accept any responsibility for death in the line of duty. However, compensation will be awarded for loss of limbs.

5-star medical care? Forget it! Pirate crews would not include a doctor, so operations would usually be carried out by the ship's carpenter or cook! 'Pass the bread knife Jim, me old mate!'

Applications can be made in person to Captain Jack Cutte-Throate at Ye Olde Shippe Inn, Plymouth harbour.

Survivors

Palm leaves drooped lazily in the warm air. Rippling waves lapped at the golden sand. Distant squawks signalled that the jungle was waking up to a new day. The first rays of sun peeped over the hills, gradually revealing the motionless figures that lay there beneath the trees.

One of the shapes stirred. It sat up. It opened its mouth. "Look at the state of my hair! Just *look* at it! **And where's my breakfast?!**"

If anyone heard, they didn't show it. They'd already put up with two full days of non-stop moaning. Shutting their ears to the whining voice, they rolled over and went back to sleep.

Snow White would have to wait for her breakfast.

"Why did the publishers arrange the party for Fresh Start characters in Japan, anyway?" grumbled grumpy Shakespeare. "I mean what's wrong with London, or Stratford-upon-Avon? Somewhere that didn't involve plane travel."

"Or plane crashes," added Snow White bitterly.

"Nice place, Japan," mumbled Thog shyly. "And not that far away really."

"Maybe not for an alien from the Black Planet, who's travelled about fifty-five zillion light years just to get in on a free party!" snarled Snow White. "Besides, you might have noticed that we're not actually in Japan!"

Thog shrank back into the shadows. He'd always been bashful with females.

"I can't understand how the pilot and crew could use all the parachutes and leave us to fend for ourselves," groaned Shakespeare.

"Oh don't be so grumpy, Shakes mate," grinned Louis Squelch. "Just look at the good points. In no particular order: the trees cushioned our landing, we all survived, and now we're through to boot camp in paradise!"

"Paradise, you idiot?" snapped Snow White. "It's a jungle out there."

"That's show business, Snowy, old girl. Get used to it!"

"This is *not* show business, Louis. It's reality TV … without the cameras. There are all kinds of horrible deadly creatures just waiting for a chance to get their teeth into us!"

"Excellent!" Wild Mike rubbed his hands together in anticipation. "Bring it on!"

It was a strange group of misfits that sat on the sand to eat their meal together – trays of cold chicken pasta taken from the wrecked aircraft. Between Shakespeare and Thog sat the Cyclops, his one huge eye blinking and bloodshot from lack of sleep. Celia Smith pursed her lips in disgust. This was certainly not the quality of food she was used to – what would her TV followers think? To her left, Cake-face Jake's head dropped onto Wild Mike's shoulder, and he began to snore quietly.

"Shouldn't we send some kind of signal?" suggested Celia, when breakfast was done. "I mean they must be searching for us, surely?" She sneezed daintily into her hanky. "Drat! I wish I could get rid of this hay fever!"

"I could've called them on my mobile, if that dopey Cyclops hadn't trodden on it and crushed it!" cursed Snow White.

"It's alright for you to moan," blinked the Cyclops. "When *you* get sand in your eye, you've got another one to see out of."

"Stop snivelling!" snapped Snow White. "Wild Mike will sort your eye out. He's supposed to be good with jungle medicines."

"Oh cheer up, you two," chuckled Louis. "Celia's right. Maybe we should write a message in the sand for any passing aircraft to see."

"As the greatest writer in the history of the English language," said Shakespeare, "I feel that I should take care of that task. Want to help, Jake?"

But the only reply was a quiet snore.

"Right, let's get organised." Snow White was back where she belonged –
in control. "Cyclops, now that Wild Mike's sorted your eye problem out,
you'll be our guard. It's your job to keep your eye out for wild animals.
Thog, you'll go into the jungle with Wild Mike to find us some food. As
for you, Jake, now you've finally woken up, you can stay here and keep
the camp clean and tidy."

Jake wasn't impressed. "I don't mean to be rude, but …
er … isn't that *your* job? I mean, in all the films you've
always got a broom in your hand, sweeping up. And I'm
too tired to tidy up."

Snow White fixed Jake with a withering glare. "Who's in
charge here, Jake?" she hissed.

Jake gulped and cowered away from her. "Y-you
are, Snowy."

"Good. I'm glad we had that little chat. Now get
lost and start raiding the plane for pillows,
cooking gear and anything else that
looks as if it'll come in handy."

"What about me?" asked Celia Smith
meekly, when Jake had fled.

"You're no use to anyone while you're
sneezing your head off like that. Maybe
Wild Mike can find some kind of plant
or herb in the jungle that'll cure it. In the
meantime, just stay out of my way."

The day wore on. Eventually, in the late evening, trampling sounds were heard. Mike and Thog emerged from the jungle, carrying a wild deer and a bag full of mouth-watering fruits.

"Grub's up!" whooped Mike. "Celia, get cooking!"

"Good idea," said Snow White. "Wake Jake up. He can cut the fruit."

"That's odd," wondered Celia out loud. "Where *is* Jake? I haven't seen him since you sent him back to the plane."

They searched the camp. They searched the beach. They searched the trees nearby. There was no sign of Jake. He'd disappeared into the jungle.

The evening meal was not a success. While Wild Mike acted as doc and treated Celia's hay fever, Thog took over cooking duties.

"What on earth is this supposed to be?" wailed Snow White, a forkful of crispy blackened meat in her hand.

"Sorry," mumbled Thog shyly.

"Black planet, black food. I suppose it fits," she added cruelly.

Louis came to the rescue. "Don't be too harsh on poor bashful Thog. He gave 110 per cent. As our mentor you clearly chose the wrong chef."

"We're going to starve," moaned Shakespeare. "And it's all **your** fault."

"Me?! **You've** no room to talk, Mister Grumpy!" snapped Snow White. "Great job you made of that message in the sand!"

"It was poetic."

"It was rubbish! By the time any pilot finished reading it, they'd have fallen asleep at the controls. How did it start? Let's remember, shall we?

'To ye who soars, bird-like amongst the clouds,

If ye should lower thy shining eyes

And gaze down from thy lofty perch,

Thou mayst just see, marooned below …'

What's wrong with a simple '**Help!!!**' for goodness' sake?"

The reply wasn't heard. The greatest author in history had already stomped off into the jungle, never to return.

At daybreak the following morning, Wild Mike and Thog took
to the jungle on their second hunt for food. By mid-afternoon
there was still no sign of them.

"Do you think we should send out a search party?" suggested
Celia nervously.

"Consisting of who?" snarled Snow White through gritted teeth.
"A clumsy, one-eyed, dopey monster, a sneezy wimp of a TV
chef, or a ridiculously happy, grinning judge?"

"Well I don't intend to sit here and do nothing. I'm off." Picking
up her wooden spoon as a weapon, Celia stomped off towards
the trees. "You coming, Cyclops?"

"Suppose so," muttered the miserable myth.
"Someone's got to keep an eye on you."

And that was the last anyone saw of them.

Night fell. Buzzing insects circled, diving now and then to take a stinging bite.

Snow White broke the broody silence. "So, just the two of us left, eh Louis? You scared?"

"Don't be silly!" he laughed. "Someone will save us. We're famous, remember? They can't just let us die. Soon we'll be back home, safe and happy … " His voice trailed off.

"What's the matter, Louis? Why are you staring at me like that?"

"Happy … I'll be *happy.* Aha! It all adds up now."

"What all adds up? What are you on about?"

"First it was *sleepy* little Jake, then *grumpy* old Shakespeare. Next to disappear were *bashful* Thog and Wild Mike, the group's *doc.* Then *sneezy* Celia and the *dopey* Cyclops. You've driven them all away into the jungle. Now all that's left is *happy* old me." His voice rose. "Am I next on your list, Snow White? Is that your devious plan? Am I next to be voted off?"

Snow White backed away. She took one look at the mad gleam in the judge's eyes, then turned and ran for the trees.

A group of seven missing fictional characters has been found safe and well on a remote tropical island. The search continues for the eighth member of the party, a Miss S. White.

A famous writer – Shakespeare (-ous -ious -cous -cious -tious)

Green words: *Say the syllables. Say the word.*

hum'or'ous ➜ humorous   cur'i'ous ➜ curious   am'bi'tious ➜ ambitious

ad'ven'tur'ous ➜ adventurous   dan'ger'ous ➜ dangerous   pre'cious ➜ precious

hid'e'ous ➜ hideous   mur'der'ous ➜ murderous   nu'mer'ous ➜ numerous

vill'ain'ous ➜ villainous   ven'om'ous ➜ venomous   ted'i'ous ➜ tedious

de'li'cious ➜ delicious

Say the root word. Say the whole word.   poison ➜ poisonous   jealous ➜ jealousy

Red words: these   they   were   want   was   where   there   some   thought

Challenge words: young   serious   plague   characters   theatre   dictionaries

Vocabulary check: **inhabitants** *people who live in a place*   **loathsome** *causing hatred, repulsive*   **rascally** *a cheeky person*   **knave** *a dishonest man*

Mission impossible! (-able -ably -ible -ibly)

Green words: *Say the syllables. Say the word.*

im'poss'ible ➜ impossible   terr'ible ➜ terrible   un'stable ➜ unstable

un'rea ch'able ➜ unreachable   im'pass'able ➜ impassable   un'climb'able ➜ unclimbable

un'bear'able ➜ unbearable   un'pre'dict'able ➜ unpredictable   un'rel'i'able ➜ unreliable

en'able ➜ enable   con'sid'er'able ➜ considerable   in'cred'ible ➜ incredible

Say the root word. Say the whole word.

sensible ➜ sensibly   unbelievable ➜ unbelievably   uncomfortable ➜ uncomfortably

Red words: there   could   brought   would   through

Challenge words:

Jose   seriously   routine   journey   wearing   earned   interviews   guests   honour

Vocabulary check: **refuge** *safe shelter*   **foreman** *supervisor who directs other workers*   **rationed** *divided up to stop supplies from running out*   **simulate** *pretend to be like something*

Pirate application pack (-tion -sion -ssion)

Green words: *Say the syllables. Say the word.*

app'li'ca'tion ➜ application   in'for'ma'tion ➜ information

qual'i'fi'ca'tions ➜ qualifications   ed'u'ca'tion ➜ education

su'per'sti'tions ➜ superstitions   des'crip'tion ➜ description

in'struc'tions ➜ instructions   ex'cep'tion ➜ exception   el'ec'tion ➜ election

de'ci'sion ➜ decision   reg'u'la'tions ➜ regulations   con'fis'ca'tion ➜ confiscation

pro'vi'sions ➜ provisions   o'cca'sion ➜ occasion   pro'tec'tion ➜ protection

a'ccomm'o'da'tion ➜ accommodation   con'di'tions ➜ conditions

com'pen'sa'tion ➜ compensation   op'er'a'tions ➜ operations

Red words:

one   was   would   they   other   their   could   were

Challenge words:

young   brought   board   during   periods   calm   trouble   obey   receive   guilty

island   mouldy   tough   biscuit   swords   sardines

Vocabulary check: **superstitions** *beliefs that are not based on evidence*   **irritable** *easily annoyed*   **obey** *to follow a command*   **regulations** *rules made by someone in authority*   **confiscation** *taking away someone's property*   **marooning** *leaving someone trapped and alone*   **infested** *overrun, invaded*   **compensation** *something awarded to someone for their pain or suffering*

Survivors – an extended read

Challenge words:

warm   squawks   characters   cushioned   business   group   eye   guard   fruits

Vocabulary check: **bashful** *shy*   **anticipation** *expecting something*   **pursed** *make a rounded shape with your lips*   **raid** *taking or stealing something*   **ye** *old English word meaning 'you' (plural)*   **thy** *old English word meaning 'your'*   **thou** *old English word meaning 'you' (singular)*   **mayst** *old English word meaning 'may'*   **devious** *underhand, shifty*   **remote** *distant, away from large numbers of people*